Ri

by Iain Gray

Lang**Syne**

PUBLISHING

WRITING *to* REMEMBER

LangSyne

PUBLISHING

WRITING *to* REMEMBER

Vineyard Business Centre,
Pathhead, Midlothian EH37 5XP
Tel: 01875 321 203 Fax: 01875 321 233
E-mail: info@lang-syne.co.uk
www.langsyneshop.co.uk

Design by Dorothy Meikle
Printed by Ricoh Print Scotland
© Lang Syne Publishers Ltd 2010

ISBN 978-1-85217-351-7

Ritchie

MOTTO:
Honour is acquired by virtue.

CREST:
The head of a unicorn.

TERRITORY:
Perthshire.

NAME variations include:
Richey
Richie
Ritchey
Richies
MacRichie
MacRitchie

Echoes of a far distant past
can still be found in most names

Chapter one:

Origins of Scottish surnames

by George Forbes

It all began with the Normans.

For it was they who introduced surnames into common usage more than a thousand years ago, initially based on the title of their estates, local villages and chateaux in France to distinguish and identify these landholdings, usually acquired at the point of a bloodstained sword.

Such grand descriptions also helped enhance the prestige of these arrogant warlords and generally glorify their lofty positions high above the humble serfs slaving away below in the pecking order who only had single names, often with Biblical connotations as in Pierre and Jacques.

The only descriptive distinctions among this peasantry concerned their occupations, like Pierre the swineherd or Jacques the ferryman.

The Normans themselves were originally Vikings (or Northmen) who raided, colonised and eventually settled down around the French coastline.

They had sailed up the Seine in their longboats in 900 AD under their ferocious leader Rollo and ruled the roost in north east France before sailing over to conquer England, bringing their relatively new tradition of having surnames with them.

It took another hundred years for the Normans to percolate northwards and surnames did not begin to appear in Scotland until the thirteenth century.

These adventurous knights brought an aura of chivalry with them and it was said no damsel of any distinction would marry a man unless he had at least two names.

The family names included that of Scotland's great hero Robert De Brus and his compatriots were warriors from families like the De Morevils, De Umphravils, De Berkelais, De Quincis, De Viponts and De Vaux.

As the knights settled the boundaries of their vast estates, they took territorial names, as in Hamilton, Moray, Crawford, Cunningham, Dunbar, Ross, Wemyss, Dundas, Galloway, Renfrew, Greenhill, Hazelwood, Sandylands and Church-hill.

Other names, though not with any obvious geographical or topographical features, nevertheless derived from ancient parishes like Douglas, Forbes, Dalyell and Guthrie.

Other surnames were coined in connection with occupations, castles or legendary deeds. Stuart originated in the word steward, a prestigious post which was an integral part of any large medieval household. The same applied to Cooks, Chamberlains, Constables and Porters.

Borders towns and forts – needed in areas like the Debateable Lands which were constantly fought over by feuding local families – had their own distinctive names; and it was often from them that the resident groups took their communal titles, as in the Grahams of Annandale, the Elliots and Armstrongs of the East Marches, the Scotts and Kerrs of Teviotdale and Eskdale.

Even physical attributes crept into surnames, as in Small, Little and More (the latter being 'beg' in Gaelic), Long or Lang, Stark, Stout, Strong or Strang and even Jolly.

Mieklejohns would have had the strength of several men, while Littlejohn was named after the legendary sidekick of Robin Hood.

Colours got into the act with Black, White, Grey, Brown and Green (Red developed into Reid,

Ruddy or Ruddiman). Blue was rare and nobody ever wanted to be associated with yellow.

Pompous worthies took the name Wiseman, Goodman and Goodall.

Words intimating the sons of leading figures were soon affiliated into the language as in Johnson, Adamson, Richardson and Thomson, while the Norman equivalent of Fitz (from the French-Latin 'filius' meaning 'son') cropped up in Fitzmaurice and Fitzgerald.

The prefix 'Mac' was 'son of' in Gaelic and clans often originated with occupations – as in MacNab being sons of the Abbot, MacPherson and MacVicar being sons of the minister and MacIntosh being sons of the chief.

The church's influence could be found in the names Kirk, Clerk, Clarke, Bishop, Friar and Monk. Proctor came from a church official, Singer and Sangster from choristers, Gilchrist and Gillies from Christ's servant, Mitchell, Gilmory and Gilmour from servants of St Michael and Mary, Malcolm from a servant of Columba and Gillespie from a bishop's servant.

The rudimentary medical profession was represented by Barber (a trade which also once included dentistry and surgery) as well as Leech or Leitch.

Businessmen produced Merchants, Mercers, Monypennies, Chapmans, Sellers and Scales, while down at the old village watermill the names that cropped up included Miller, Walker and Fuller.

Other self explanatory trades included Coopers, Brands, Barkers, Tanners, Skinners, Brewsters and Brewers, Tailors, Saddlers, Wrights, Cartwrights, Smiths, Harpers, Joiners, Sawyers, Masons and Plumbers.

Even the scenery was utilised as in Craig, Moor, Hill, Glen, Wood and Forrest.

Rank, whether high or low, took its place with Laird, Barron, Knight, Tennant, Farmer, Husband, Granger, Grieve, Shepherd, Shearer and Fletcher.

The hunt and the chase supplied Hunter, Falconer, Fowler, Fox, Forrester, Archer and Spearman.

The renowned medieval historian Froissart, who eulogised about the romantic deeds of chivalry (and who condemned Scotland as being a poverty stricken wasteland), once sniffily dismissed the peasantry of his native France as the jacquerie (or the jacques-without-names) but it was these same humble folk who ended up overthrowing the arrogant aristocracy.

In the olden days, only the blueblooded knights of antiquity were entitled to full, proper names, both Christian and surnames, but with the passing of time and a more egalitarian, less feudal atmosphere, more respectful and worthy titles spread throughout the populace as a whole.

Echoes of a far distant past can still be found in most names and they can be borne with pride in commemoration of past generations who fought and toiled in some capacity or other to make our nation what it now is, for good or ill.

Chapter two:

Brave and powerful

A surname that evolved from a forename, Ritchie is the most popular form in Scotland of Richard, Richards and Richardson.

But although the names are similar, bearers of the names have wholly different heritages.

The names stem from what was the originally Germanic forename of Richard, with 'ric' indicating 'power' and 'hard' indicating 'brave' or 'strong'.

It indicates a descent from an original Richard, or 'son of Richard', and it was popularised by those Normans who settled in England in the wake of the Norman Conquest of 1066, and subsequently in Scotland in the twelfth century at the invitation of the Scottish monarch David I.

The king had spent a great deal of his early life at the court of England's Henry I and became steeped in Anglo-Norman customs and manners.

It was when he acceded to the throne of Scotland in 1124 that he welcomed Anglo-Normans to his country, granting them lands.

Among them, in addition to great Anglo-

Norman families such as the Bruces, Frasers,
Sinclairs and many others, were 'Richards' and
'Richardsons', who through time adopted the Scottish
form of Ritchie and its variants and, in some cases,
MacRitchie.

Although the name is found today scattered
throughout Scotland, particularly in the Scottish
Borders, it was in Perthshire that the Ritchies first
established firm roots in the nation's ancient soil.

The first written record of a form of the name
in Scotland concerns a Michael Rechy, recorded in
Inverness in 1350, while a Duncan Riche held the
influential post of Sheriff of Inverness in 1512.

Seven years before that, a Duncan Ritchies is
recorded in Perth while, in 1538, a David Reche and
his wife apparently fell foul of the law in Aberdeen for
illicitly brewing beer.

In much later centuries, bearers of the Ritchie
name acquired rich honours and titles.

A Ritchie Baronetcy of Lees House was
created in 1903 for the Scot James Ritchie, who served
as Lord Mayor of London from 1903 to 1904, while
his brother Charles Ritchie was earlier created 1st
Baron Ritchie of Dundee.

Another Ritchie baronetcy was that of the

Ritchie Baronetcy of Highlands, created in 1918 for the businessman James William Ritchie.

These honours and titles were granted during comparatively peaceful times, compared to the violently turbulent times through which the Ritchies lived shortly after first becoming established in Scotland.

This was through their kinship with the mighty Clan Mackintosh, a kinship so close that, along with other clans that include those of Hardie, Hossack, MacCartney and Niven, they are considered a sept, or branch, of the clan.

As such, the history of the Ritchies over the centuries became entwined with that of the Mackintoshes, sharing in both their glorious fortunes and tragic misfortunes.

But although a sept of the Mackintoshes, whose bold motto is 'Touch not the cat without a glove' and whose crest is a mountain cat, the Ritchie independence is displayed through their own proud motto of 'Honour is acquired by virtue' and crest of the head of a unicorn.

The leading clan of the powerful confederation of clans, such as the MacPhersons, Farquharsons and Davidsons, known as Clan Chattan, the

Mackintoshes controlled a vast area from earliest times, centred on their stronghold of Inverness.

As a sept of the Mackintoshes, the Ritchies appear to have first been bloodied on the field of battle in 1263 after Viking invasion threatened when Alexander III, King of Scots, laid claim to the Hebrides.

Forewarned that Alexander was prepared to wrest the islands from Norwegian control by force if necessary, King Hakon of Norway embarked with a mighty fleet that sailed from Bergen in July of 1263.

His fierce band of battle-hardened sea raiders plundered and ravaged Kintyre, Bute and Islay, before appearing off the west coast mainland township of Largs.

A storm blew many of the vessels onto the shore beneath overhanging hills on the night of September 30, and there was a skirmish the following morning between a band of Norsemen attempting to salvage their cargo and a force that had been hastily raised by Alexander from all over Scotland to repel the invasion.

Included in this force was a band of Mackintoshes and kinsfolk that included a number of Ritchies.

King Hakon ordered a further attempt to retrieve the cargo the following day, resulting in the battle of Largs, a battle in which the Mackintosh chief was killed.

But the Norsemen were driven back to their vessels and King Hakon died a few weeks later in Kirkwall, Orkney, and the battle is commemorated annually at Largs with the ceremonial burning of a Viking longboat.

The Ritchies and their Mackintosh kinsmen were back on the bloody field of battle during Scotland's bitter War of Independence with England, most notably at Bannockburn in June of 1314.

This was when a 20,000-strong English army under Edward II was defeated by a Scots army less than half this strength, and led by the great warrior King Robert the Bruce.

By midsummer of 1313 the forbidding fortress of Stirling Castle was occupied by an English garrison under the command of Sir Philip Mowbray.

Bruce's brother, Edward, agreed to a pledge by Mowbray that if the castle was not relieved by battle by midsummer of the following year, then he would surrender; this made battle almost inevitable, and by June 23 of 1314 the two armies faced one another at Bannockburn, in sight of the castle.

It was on this day that Bruce famously slew the arrogant English knight Sir Henry de Bohun in single combat, but the battle proper was not fought until the following day.

The English cavalry launched a desperate but futile charge on the densely packed ranks of Scottish spearmen known as schiltrons, but the Scots fought bravely, with the Mackintosh chief Angus Mackintosh leading his clan and loyal kinsfolk such as the Ritchies.

The English army was totally routed, and Scotland's independence had been secured, to the glory of Bruce and those who fought for him.

One of the most unusual engagements in which the Mackintoshes and their kinsfolk took part was more a gladiatorial contest than a battle.

This was in 1396 when a Clan Chattan contingent took part in the famous Battle of the Clans, staged on a large, flat meadow on the outskirts of Perth known as the North Inch.

A bitter feud had dragged out for some time between the clan and Clan Kay, a bloody vendetta that had not only visited mayhem on the clans themselves, but also periodically devastated the lives of their more peaceful neighbours.

In a desperate bid to resolve the matter, the king, Robert III, arranged for a fight to the death between the two warring factions, watched by not only the monarch himself but a glittering array of courtiers and even the Dauphin of France.

Sixty champions were chosen from each side and, armed with a fierce arsenal of swords, dirks and axes, and allowed to shoot off one volley of crossbow bolts, the 120 warriors battled it out until only eleven Chattans were left standing on the blood-soaked field of combat.

The sole Kay survivor wisely took to his heels and swam for safety across the River Tay.

Chapter three:

A royal cause

In decidedly more serious conflicts than that of the late fourteenth century Battle of the Clans, the Ritchies, through their kinship with Clan Mackintosh, became embroiled in the ultimately futile cause of the Royal House of Stuart.

A bitter civil war raged in Scotland between 1638 and 1649 between the forces of those Presbyterian Scots who had signed a National Covenant that opposed the divine right of the Stuart monarchy and Royalists such as James Graham, 1st Marquis of Montrose, whose prime allegiance was to Charles I.

Although Montrose had initially supported the Covenant, his conscience later forced him to switch sides and his great campaigns were fought between 1644 and 1645.

This was a year that became known as the Year of Miracles because of the brilliant military successes of Montrose and his allies such as the Mackintoshes and their kinsmen.

At the battle of Inverlochy, fought on

February 2, 1645, the Earl of Argyll was forced to ignominiously flee in his galley after 1,500 of his Covenanters were wiped out in a surprise attack.

What made this victory all the more notable was that Montrose's forces had arrived at Inverlochy after an exhausting 36-hour march south through knee-deep snow from the area of present day Fort Augustus.

Another great victory followed at Kilsyth on August 15, 1645, but final defeat came at Philiphaugh, near Selkirk, less than a month later; betrayed and captured five years later, Montrose was executed in Edinburgh for treason.

Following the flight into exile of the Stuart monarch James II (James VII of Scotland) in 1688, the Protestant William of Orange and his wife Mary succeeded to the throne.

Jacobites, as supporters of the exiled Royal House of Stuart were known, raised the banner of revolt in 1715 following the succession to the throne of George, the Elector of Hanover.

One of the main leaders of the revolt, the Earl of Mar, raised the Stuart Standard at Braemar and, despite mustering a force of no less than 10,000 men, including Mackintoshes and their kinsmen, the

Jacobite cause was effectively lost after the battle of Sheriffmuir, in November of 1715, when Mar withdrew his forces north to Perth.

The Rising had fizzled out, but the Stuart Standard was raised again thirty years later when Prince Charles Edward Stuart, son of the exiled James III (James VIII of Scotland) arrived on Scottish shores.

Landing on the small Outer Hebridean island of Eriskay on July 22, 1745, he stepped foot on the mainland three days later; the Stuart Standard was raised on August 19, at Glenfinnan, on Loch Shiel, followed by victory in September at the battle of Prestonpans.

The confident prince and his Jacobite army set off on the long march south to London to claim what was believed to be the rightful Stuart inheritance of the throne, but reached only as far as Derby before the controversial decision was taken in early December to withdraw back over the border.

When the rebellion had broken out the Mackintosh chief, Angus Mackintosh, had been firmly on the side of the Government, away from home serving as a commander in the Black Watch.

But his wife, the feisty Jacobite Lady Anne Farquharson-Mackintosh, raised 350 men from the

Clan Chattan Confederation, and it was the Mackintoshes and their kinsfolk such as the Ritchies who led the first charge on the Government troops at the battle of Culloden, fought on Drumossie Moor, near Inverness, on April 16, 1746.

But Jacobite hopes were dashed forever in what proved to be the last major battle fought on British soil – with hundreds of clansmen left dead on the battlefield and hundreds of others dying later from their wounds and the brutal treatment of their government captors.

Away from the clamour of battle, Dr Joseph Ritchie was the English explorer, surgeon and naturalist who was born in 1788.

He set off in 1818 along with George Francis Lyon and Sir John Barrow on an ambitious but abortive expedition to Africa to find the course of the River Niger and the location of what was then the legendary Timbuktu.

But the expedition was badly funded and organised, and Ritchie fell ill and died less than a year later.

One prominent nineteenth century Scot of the Ritchie name was the leading philosopher David Ritchie, born in 1853 in Jedburgh, in the Borders.

His father, George Ritchie, was the Jedburgh minister who was elected Moderator of the General Assembly of the Church of Scotland in 1870; described by his peers as 'a man of scholarship and culture', he nevertheless had rather odd views on child-rearing – not allowing his young son to make friends or play with other boys.

He therefore led a rather solitary existence as a lad, and it is this that is considered to have concentrated his mind from an early age on intellectual pursuits.

A brilliant scholar, he was aged only 16 when he graduated in Classics from Edinburgh University.

There then followed further study at Balliol College, Oxford, where he was later appointed as a tutor, before his return north of the border in 1894 as professor of metaphysics at St Andrews University, a post he held until his death in 1903.

One of the foremost philosophers of his age, the Scot was a founder of the prestigious Aristotelian Society, which flourishes to this day, and served as its third professor from 1898 to 1899.

Ritchies have also contributed to the field of journalism, most notably in the form of the Scots William Ritchie, born in 1781 in Lundin Links, and his brother John, born in 1778.

From a humble background, the older brother, John, worked for a time on a local farm before moving to Edinburgh and embarking on a career in the drapery business; he was followed later to the capital by William, to study at Edinburgh University and pursue a career in law.

But, very much politically aware and concerned with the state of Britain's affairs in general and those of Scotland in particular, the brothers, along with two others that included the customs official Charles Maclaren, launched their own independent newspaper, *The Scotsman*, in 1817.

With its pledge for 'impartiality, firmness and independence', it was not long before the newspaper, which began as a weekly before becoming a daily, attracted howls of outraged protest from the Establishment and the less independently minded rival newspapers of the time. But *The Scotsman* thrived, and survives to this day.

William Ritchie was the newspaper's first editor; he died in 1831, and his brother John carried on as owner until his own death in 1870.

Many bearers of the Ritchie name found new lives for themselves on foreign shores, to the benefit of those lands in which they settled.

Sir William Ritchie, who was born in 1813 in Annapolis, Nova Scotia, and who died in 1895, served as Chief Justice of the Supreme Court of Canada from 1879 to 1892.

The distinguished judge, who died in 1892, was a grandson of a Glasgow-born merchant, John Ritchie, who settled in Nova Scotia in the late eighteenth century.

In the field of diplomacy, Charles Ritchie, born in Halifax, Nova Scotia, in 1906 and also a descendant of John Ritchie, was the Canadian diplomat and diarist who served as Canada's ambassador to West Germany from 1954 to 1958 and ambassador to the United States from 1962 to 1966.

Ambassador to the North Atlantic Council for a time and Canadian High Commissioner to the United Kingdom from 1967 to 1971, the diplomat is also renowned for his best-selling published diaries, including the 1974 *The Siren Years*.

Made a Companion of the Order of Canada in 1969, he died in 1995.

Chapter four:

On the world stage

From film and sport to music and the military, generations of bearers of the Ritchie name, in all its diverse spellings, have gained distinction through a variety of pursuits and endeavours.

In the world of film, **Guy Ritchie** is the English filmmaker and screenwriter who was born in 1968 in Hatfield, Hertfordshire, and whose first successful feature film was the 1998 *Lock, Stock and Two Smoking Barrels*.

The movie won an Edgar Award from the Mystery Writers of America for Best Motion Picture Screenplay, while his other films include the 2005 *Revolver* and the 2009 *Sherlock Holmes*.

It was while working on *Lock, Stock and Two Smoking Barrels* that he first met the American singer and actress Madonna; the couple married at Skibo Castle in Scotland in 2000, but divorced nine years later.

Also behind the camera lens was American film director **Michael Ritchie**, born in Wisconsin in 1938 and whose films include the 1969 *Downhill*

Racer, *Prime Cut*, from 1972, and the 1995 *The Fantasticks*; he died in 2001.

Born in North Dakota in 1938, **Clint Ritchie** was the American actor who, although appearing in a number of films that included *Earthquake*, *The St Valentine's Day Massacre* and *Patton*, is best remembered for his role from 1979 as Clint Buchanan in the long-running American television soap *One Life*; the actor died in 2009.

Born to Irish parents in London in 1964, Shane Roche is the actor better known by his stage name of **Shane Richie**, and for his role for a time as Alfie Moon in the BBC television soap *EastEnders*.

Also in the world of television soaps, **Kate Ritchie** is the award-winning Australian actress, born in 1978 in Goulburn, New South Wales, who played the character of Sally Fletcher in *Home and Away* from 1988 to 2008.

In the competitive world of sport, **Darren Ritchie** is the Scottish athlete who was born in Edinburgh in 1975.

Scottish Long Jump Champion on six occasions, at the time of writing his experience is being put to use as the Scottish Athletics National Jumps and Combined Events Manager.

In ice hockey, **Byron Ritchie**, born in 1977 in Burnaby, British Columbia, is the Canadian professional player who played for teams that include the Hartford Whalers and the Carolina Hurricanes before joining Russian team Dinamo Minsk.

Ritchies have also proved talented on the fields of European football, with **Andy Ritchie**, born in Manchester in 1960, having played for top teams that include Manchester United and Leeds United, while another **Andy Ritchie** is the former Scottish midfielder who played for teams that include Celtic and Motherwell.

Born in 1956 in Bellshill, Lanarkshire, he also played for a time with Greenock Morton, his prolific goal scoring earning him the nickname of "The King of Cappielow Park."

Born in Kettering in 1941, **John Ritchie** was the English striker who has the distinction of having been Stoke City's top goal scorer to date, scoring 176 goals in 343 games during two spells with the club; he died in 2007.

His namesake, **John Ritchie**, born in 1947 in Auchterderran, is the former Scottish goalkeeper who played for teams that include Dundee United and Bradford City.

On the cricket pitch, **Greg Ritchie** is the former Australian cricketer, born in 1960 in Stanthorpe, Queensland; nicknamed "Fat Cat", he played first- class cricket for his native state and in 30 Tests between 1982 and 1987.

In baseball, **Todd Ritchie** is the former Major League pitcher, born in 1971 in Portsmouth, Virginia, who played for teams that include the Minnesota Twins and the Tampa Bay Devil Rays, while on the tennis court **Josiah Ritchie** was a top British player of the early twentieth century.

Born in 1870 in London, he won not only a gold medal in the men's singles at the 1908 Olympics, but also a silver in the men's doubles and a bronze in the men's indoor singles; he died in 1955.

In the creative world of music, **Lionel Richie** is the top-selling American singer, songwriter and record producer born in 1949 in Tuskegee, Alabama.

He is also a leading activist for the diagnosis and treatment of breast cancer – inspired by his grand-mother, who was diagnosed with the disease when aged in her '80s but who lived until the age of 104.

Graduating with a degree in economics from the Tuskegee Institution, he later turned his attention to music, releasing a self-titled album in 1982 that contained the international hit *Truth*; other hits include the 1985 *Say You, Say Me*, the 1984 *Hello* and, from 2008, *Just Go*.

He is also the adoptive father of the American actress, singer, television personality and socialite **Nicole Richie**; born in 1981, she is best known for her role in the American reality television series *The Simple Life*, along with fellow socialite Paris Hilton, and also for her role in the 2005 film *Kids in America*.

Better known by his adoptive punk rock name of **Sid Vicious**, John Ritchie, born in London in 1957, was the bassist with the controversial British band the Sex Pistols.

The musician died from a heroin overdose in New York in February of 1979, shortly after being released on bail while facing a charge of allegedly stabbing his girlfriend Nancy Spungen to death.

In a rather less controversial musical genre, **Jean Ritchie** is the veteran American folksinger, songwriter and dulcimer player born in Kentucky in 1922, and whose albums include the 1952 *Traditional Songs of Her Kentucky Mountain Home* and the 1997 *Childhood Songs*.

In politics, **Albert Ritchie**, born in 1876 in Richmond, Virginia, and who died in 1936, was the

American Democratic Party politician who served as 49th Governor of Maryland from 1920 to 1935; he also made two unsuccessful bids, in 1924 and 1932, for the Democratic presidential nomination.

Bearers of the name have also distinguished themselves in times of conflict, not least **Henry Ritchie**, who was awarded the Victoria Cross, the highest award for bravery in the face of the enemy for British and Commonwealth troops.

Born in Edinburgh in 1876, he received one of the first VCs awarded to naval personnel during the First World War for his actions in aiding commandos on a raid on what was then the German colonial harbour of Dar-es-Salaam shortly after the outbreak of the war in 1914; he died in 1958.

Another Scottish recipient of the Victoria Cross during the First World War was **Walter Ritchie**, born in Glasgow in 1892.

He had been a drummer in the 2nd Battalion, The Seaforth Highlanders, when, during the First Battle of the Somme in July of 1916, he rallied his comrades to launch a successful assault on an enemy trench; later achieving the rank of Drum-Major, he died in 1965.

During the Second World War, **General Sir**

Neil Ritchie, born in 1897, was the British army officer who held a number of senior staff posts and commands, including for a time the command of the Eighth Army in North Africa.

Colonel of the Black Watch for a time after the war, and the recipient of many awards that included Knight Grand Cross of the Order of the British Empire, the Military Cross and the Legion of Honour, he died in Toronto in 1983 after immigrating to Canada.

During the American Civil War of 1861 to 1865, **John Ritchie** was the prominent Union Army general who had earlier been instrumental in opposing the expansion of slavery in the territory of Kansas.

Taking to the air, **Brigadier-General Richard "Steve" Ritchie**, born in 1942 in North Carolina, is a former United States Air Force pilot, Vietnam veteran and recipient of the Air Force Cross.

One bearer of the Ritchie name who had a particularly inventive turn of mind was **Edward Samuel Ritchie**, born in 1814 in Massachusetts.

By the time of his death in 1895, the physicist had contributed greatly to the science of navigation through the invention of a number of devices that included a special naval compass.

In contemporary times and keeping up the Ritchie inventive tradition, **Dennis Ritchie** is the American computer scientist who was born in 1941 in Bronxville, New York.

The recipient of a number of scientific awards, he is internationally recognised for his influence on a number of computer programming languages and operating systems such as UNIX.

The Ritchie name is also to be found on the landscape, with **Ritchie County** located in the American state of West Virginia and named in honour of a newspaper publisher, William Ritchie, while, on the oceans, **Ritchie's Archipelago** is a group of small islands in the Bay of Bengal.